JASON DANIELS

COURAGE TO START

The Ultimate Guide on How to Have Courage to Face Anything and Confidence to Achieve Your Dreams

Descrierea CIP a Bibliotecii Naţionale a României
JASON DANIELS
    COURAGE TO START. The Ultimate Guide on How to Have Courage to Face Anything and Confidence to Achieve Your Dreams / Jason Daniels – Bucharest: Editura My Ebook, 2021
    ISBN

JASON DANIELS

COURAGE TO START

**The Ultimate Guide on How to Have Courage to Face
Anything and Confidence to Achieve Your Dreams**

My Ebook Publishing House
Bucharest, 2021

CONTENTS

INTRODUCTION

Fear may come in numerous forms and it's crucial to comprehend what it is. There's unhealthy fear and healthy fear. Well, never don't fret as there are answers to help you right here.

Chapter 1

The Meaning Of Being Frightened

Synopsis

When we're frightened of something that can't really harm us - like spiders - or something we may do nothing about - like old age - then our fear is unhealthy, for it only makes us distressed.

But, when someone stops smoking since they're afraid of getting lung cancer, this is a healthy fear.

The Basics

We have several fears-fears of act of terrorism, fear of passingaway, fear of being apart from individuals we love; fear of losing our job, the list is perpetual! Many our fears are rooted in delusions- confused ways of viewing ourselves and the world around us. If we learn take control, and relax and finally wipe out these delusions, the unhealthy, is annihilated.

Even so, we need the healthy fear. For example, there's no point in a smoker becoming terrified of dying of lung cancer unless there's something that he or she will do about it, i.e. stop smoking. If a smoker has a sufficient fear of passing away of lung cancer, he or she will adopt steps to kick the habit.

Even as a smoker is vulnerable to lung cancer due to smokes, it's true that we're vulnerable to risk and harm, we're vulnerable to ageing, sickness, and pains that come from the delusions of bonds,wrath, and ignorance.

We might choose to live in self-denial and thereby give up what control we have, or we may choose to recognize this vulnerability, admit that we're in danger, and so determine a way to avoid the risk by removing the real causes of all fear (the same as the smokes). In this way we gain control, and if we're in control we have no cause for fear.

A balanced fear is healthy as it serves to cue constructive action to avoid a true danger. We only need fear as an impulse till we have removed the causes of our vulnerability through attaining spirituality, inner peace and gradually strengthening the mind. Once we do this, we're fearless as we no longer have anything that may hurt us.

Staying afraid of things we don't have control over is unhealthy fear, a survival mechanism failed. Sometimes this can be healthy and normal. However fear has become rampant when it neverleaves us. It becomes a shadow, forever alongside you.

Fear crushes self-reliance, enthusiasm, and initiative. It promotes procrastination, and leads to weak character. It defeats love, fogs memories, and finally leads to misery and sadness.

However take heart, for a lack of courage is nothing more than a state of mind. It may be mastered.

Chapter 2

What You Might Fear

Synopsis

Have you ever felt like fear was keeping you from achieving your entire potential in life? If so, you're surely not alone as fearfulness is among the biggest obstacles that a lot of people confront when trying to acquire a better life.

Below are some of the many ways that fearfulness might hold you back:

What's Holding You Back

Now and again fearfulness might make even the littlest changes seem extremely uncomfortable. For example, you could be deeply dissatisfied with your career, but feel anxious or unsure about finding a better one.

Or you could have always dreamed of buying your own home but fret that the responsibility could be too much to deal with.

Fearfulness might prevent you from breaking bad habits.

We all know that smoking, poor dietary choices, unreasonable alcohol and a sedentary life-style are a formula for unhealthiness, but we frequently continue these habits as they help numb our nervous or awful feelings.

If you've ever tried to break a foul habit like this, you understand how nerve-racking it might be as suddenly you're filled with anxiousness and you don't know how to handle it.

Fearfulness might prevent you from taking risks. Many of us shy away from risk, as we fear bad results. For example, you could hesitate about investing, as you fear losing money, or don't go into a new relationship as you were hurt by the last one.

What many of us fail to realize is that risk might bring excellentpayoffs. Avoiding risk may help us prevent negative results but wealso miss the excitement and joy that come from positive results.

Fearfulness may prevent you from chasing your goals.

Have you ever dreamed of doing something exceptional but were never able to push yourself to achieve it? Perhaps you dreamed of being a comedian but feared the thought of public speaking, or you wanted to be a best selling author but were too frightened to compose that novel.

Fearfulness might prevent you from expanding your life. Social anxiety is another basic way that fearfulness might limit your potential. It may prevent you from attending gatherings so your career or business won't grow decently.

It's essential to note that many of these fears are often unfounded. They're simply a sensing that things might go wrong - but that doesn'tmean they will. Rather than attempting to force your way through the fear, you may find it easier to explore ways that fearfulness might be done away with.

When you realize how to handle the fearfulness, you merely handle it as you would any minor obstacle and then continue on your way to producing the best life you possibly can.

Chapter 3

Exposing Your Fears

Synopsis

Fears have to be disclosed in order for them to be addressed. We all have fears. Even those that appear to be really confident might have fears that they're failing to manage. At times these fears lead to aggressive behaviors and other times they lead to timidity and lack of poise and confidence.

Have A Look

Many people have fears from childhood or adult life that they don't directly remember but which have a massive affect on how they lead their lives daily and on how they arrive at decisions.

A few people have fears that they're clearly aware of but have no clue how to deal with and how to break the bad affect they're having on their lives. Fear has its space in your life but uncontrolled fear can lead to a life of sorrow, self denigration and unfulfilled goals and desires.

Think of when you were a youngster and simply knew there was a monster lurking at the foot of your bed? How did you control that fear? In all probability someone turned on the lights and remarked that your monster was nothing more than a coat a chair. Once the lights came on, the monster was no longer dreaded.

The same thing applies to defeating our fear in adulthood. If we view our fear in the light of day, we discover that what we're afraid of isn't so atrocious after all.

Understand all the same that fear is your enemy - no other way to describe it. I'm not discussing that innate life preserving action along with a boost of adrenaline that happens if an animal is coming at you. I'm discussing the fears people live with daily.

Fear is your foe. Someone once distinguished fear as, Sand in the machinery of life. Fear doesn't help you, it shackles you. Fear doesn't get you outside; it holds you inside. Fear never helps you put your best foot forward; it simply keeps both of your feet in cement.

Learn to accept your fears, embrace your fears.

But first of all you have to expose your fears. This will be hard work and time consuming, but the advantages will be enormous.

Take a moment to write down your fears. Start with your aim in life on the top of the sheet, and then let your ideas flow underneath and don't stop till you've found each and every one.

Chapter 4

Get Moving

Synopsis

Fears and inner suffering won't go away on their own. The danger here is, naturally, that many will use it as a different excuse. Inner work becomes a different obstacle, a different reason to remain in a rut rather than doing anything.

Some of the times, the best way to defeat fear is to simply do it.

Get Out Of Your Rut

We can take some tips from some well respected experts.

If you are in a rut, not being able to take action, using this formula will be hugely helpful. It can be used in so many ways - to begin exercising again after a long layoff, to cut back procrastination, and even to better relationships and of course deal with fear- A 5% Statement

A 5% statement is split into 2 halves. Examples would be:
If I were to be 5% more responsible today, I would __.

If I were to be 5% less tentative now, I would__.

Here was one I wrote up: If I was 5% more giving today, I'd buy a homeless person lunch and spend time visiting with them over lunch.

Stop, and think about your particular excuse, fear, or failing. What would you require? What would the first half of your statement be?

After that, make out the statement each morning when you wake. The action you have to take might change daily, however regardless of what you do, your life will continue going in the right direction.

The wisdom in this is obvious, for attempting to change overnight is literally impossible. It would incite much inner resistance. 5% increments are enough, and there will be reduced resistance.

When momentum begins, from time to time the trouble comes in stopping!

Another technique for getting ourselves into action is to list the price and the benefits of staying on our present path.

The price: keep up with a list of this, and carry it around all day. Does it make you worried? Does it keep you working at a job you don't like? Does it keep you lonely? What would happen in 5, 10, or 20 years if you continued going down your present path?

Read this list whenever you're able to.

The advantages: What do you get out of not living up to your potential? Maybe your acquaintances and loved ones are giving you emotional backing and a lot of care when you complain of your misery. Perhaps you might want to move to a different city to pursue your passion, and you don't want to have to go through the trouble. Maybe you don't feel you have the skills to make new friends once you move.

Write everything down so you can examine your patterns.

Again, these exercises might seem to be a lot of work - but please realize that a hesitance to journal and investigate yourself is the same hesitance that holds you back for your fear. Possibly finishing this work might be the first in a 5% statement to get you moving in the right direction.

Chapter 5

Use Affirmations

Synopsis

Something that helps me is this affirmation: "there's no fearfulness, there's just God", but you have to be a believer to use this strategy, if not in "God", in Divine Order and Wisdom.

It's truly potent as it puts you in touch with that greater order and wisdom that molds the universe, in which there's no fearfulness. It feels truly soothing and helps you feel peaceful, steady and grounded inside.

I use favorable affirmations on a day-to-day basis (I'm programmed for success) When a person understands what fearfulness really isthey might overcome fearfulness easily.

You've the limitless power of your brain to adjust anything negative and do anything you want in life. Fearfulness might only exist if you allow it.

Changing It

Affirmations are like affirmative prayers, except you are not addressing them to the universe, but simply reciting favorable statements with the aim to shift your focus from fearfulness to love, peace, joy, self-confidence, or any other empowering feeling.

For affirmations to be truly effective, they have to repeated frequently throughout the day - or even better, on an ongoing basis for longer periods.

You are able to use affirmations written by other people or write your own. Writing your own affirmations is easier than you might think. Simply consider the feeling you want the affirmation to activate inside you and word the statement so that it's in present tense.

For example, if you feel anxious about an approaching meeting, you could develop an affirmation that states: "I feel relaxed, confident and centered". Say this affirmation over and over till you truly do begin to feel relaxed, confident and centered.

One common issue with this: your subconscious may feel resistant and keep coming back to the reasons why you are frightened. Therefore, you'll engage in a kind of tug of war with your subconscious where you go on saying how relaxed and confident you feel, and your subconscious keeps responding, "You are so full of it! You know you're really scared!"

If this happens, you will be able to feel it because the affirmation will feel like a lie every time you recite it. If you go on saying it anyway, you'll likely feel increasingly more nervous as you go along.

One effective resolution is to turn your affirmation into a statement of choice. Instead of saying, "I feel relaxed, confident and focused," you might say, "I choose to feel relaxed and centered." This helps short- circuit your subconscious objections, as you are not denying your fearful feelings; you are merely recognizing that you choose to feel otherwise.

Another solution is to relieve the pressure you feel by concentrating on a gradual process of transformation, rather than saying the affirmation as fact. Illustration: "With every passing moment I'm feeling less agitated and more in control." Or, "I'm beginning to feel a bit less excited now".

If you find that you are still struggling to make affirmations work for you, there's yet a different option that might be effective when the others have failed. Try stating what you WANT, rather than caring about what you don't want.

For example, "I want to go into that meeting feeling quite self- confident, quite centered and really resourceful. I want to know instinctively how to address the questions I'll be asked, and I wish to leave the meeting feeling like I made a solid positive impression."

As you say these words, try to tune into the feelings of what you are saying. Imagine feeling proud of yourself, positive in your abilities, and recognizing that the meeting went well. This process ought to have a favorable effect on your state of mind as you'll have strengthened your vision of the outcome you want, rather than continuing to perpetuate the fearfulness.

An excellent way to speed up your success with affirmations is to make use of modern technology.

You may utilize audio that contains an affirmation sequence that when listened to while being guided into a deep meditative state, will help in the re-programming of your unconscious brain to block unwanted thought and behavior.

As you let the audio work, you'll be furthering the ongoing acceptance of fresh and favorable ways of thinking, acting and living.

Chapter 6

Self Hypnosis And Reprogramming

Synopsis

Everyone feels fearfulness. Whether it's the fearfulness of high places, fearfulness of flying, fearfulness of public speaking or the fearfulness of spiders, all these fears and phobias may be foiled for good with hypnosis.

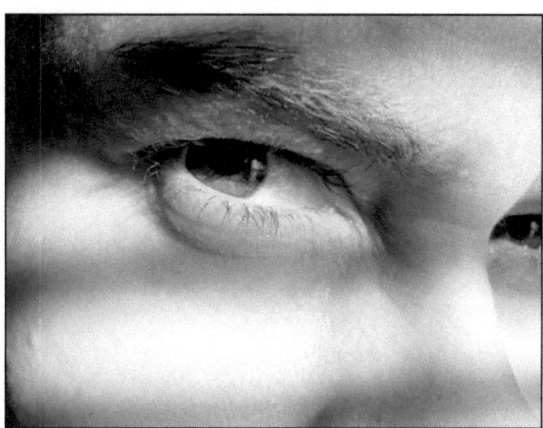

Great Techniques

Self-hypnosis is an extremely suggestible state wherein the individual may send suggestions to himself. It's easy to figure out that the operation involves providing yourself with suggestions, rather than receiving them from a different individual.

Our brain is a really powerful instrument and hypnosis may effectively help you rewire your past views and notions. Since hypnosis is a non-invasive strategy of treatment, it's safe and gentle enough for anyone to use. The process will allow you to relax your brain and get at the core issue that's causing fearfulness and phobia to demonstrate in your life. If your fears are beaten, you develop confidence, increase your self-esteem and become more positive.

You're able to either utilize self hypnosis to treat your fearfulness, or you may go to a professional hypnotherapist. If you choose to go it alone, it's frequently helpful to use a recorded hypnosis session in order to direct you through the mental process. You're able to make this recording yourself or you may buy a session on CD or an MP3 format.

The procedure of hypnosis is easy. You or your hypnotherapist will relax your brain by a series of breaths and counting. Once you're in a hypnotic state you will be able to dig into your brain for the central cause of your fearfulness or phobia.

Hypnosis lets you access the subconscious part of your brain which acts as a storage of your previous experiences. Here you'll be able to find what is causing your fearfulness, and replace those feelings of nervousness with confident and empowering statements.

For instance, instead of using "I'm no longer afraid of meeting people" you'd program yourself with a suggestion that states "I'm confident and unafraid if I meet new people."

Processing with hypnosis helps you get rid of your past mental programming and gives you fresh suggestions will help you with overcoming fears.

You might likewise actually rewrite your fears into something much more encouraging. Remember that fear is your body's natural response to what you trust is a threatening situation. On the other hand, if you choose to believe that there's nothing to fear, your body will have no reason to react.

If you've attempted to relax your body and mentally stay in the moment but can't seem to shake the feelings of fear and

28

anxiety, you may try deliberately revising your experience so that it has another outcome than the one you fear.

A different approach is to kick it up a notch and turn your thoughtsin a more empowering direction. As soon as you notice that you're starting to veer into negative thinking stop yourself at once and engage in some empowering self-talk.

Or you may strengthen your belief that you're able to handle any outcome at all.

Finally, you might create a game in which you come up with the very best result you might imagine - regardless how bizarre it might be.

Develop the most outlandish, funny, or inspiring outcomes you might imagine, and in no time at all you'll feel the fear blowing over and your heart lifting. The most essential part of utilizing these variations is to shake free from the illusion of fearful possibilities and remind yourself that fear is simply an emotional reaction triggered by your own thoughts. Changing your thoughts will likewise alter the emotional reaction.

Chapter 7

Confidence is a Mental Attitude

Synopsis

It might sound commonplace, but now is really the 1st day of the remainder of your life!

Confidence is a mental attitude, which will let you have confident, yet honest opinions of yourself and your states of affairs. When you have confidence, you'll believe on your own powers, and have a universal sense of command over your life. You'll think that, within reason, you'll be able to accomplish what you wish to do.

Attitude

Confidence is a mental attitude that's learned with experiences. Once you undergo success, you'll tend to anticipate being successful. And that notion of anticipation will cause you to have a feeling of self- confidence.

For instance: A young fellow wishes to learn how to be a boxer, so he acquires lessons, and acquires a coach.

His coach won't put him into the ring till he has accumulated adequate stamina and skill. And even then, the coach will only put him up against a rival that he recognizes his fighter may beat. When his fighter beats the adversary, he's successful, and begins to realize confidence in his abilities.

With every contest, the coach puts his fighter up against an adversary who's a slimly better fighter then the last, but not great enough to trounce his man. By the finish of the 3rd fight, the young boxer starts to expect to win his 4th, and so his self-confidence continues to develop. This scenario goes forward to repeat itself. And as long as the fighter succeeds, his expectations of success, and his feelings of confidence will go on to grow.

Conceive of how your life would be better if you felt confident. First of all, sit back and take a couple of minutes to let yourself relax. If you understand how to do progressive relaxation, then you ought to go ahead and do that. Or, you are able to download something off the net.

Or merely fantasize a relaxing experience. Do you like the beach? If you do, then make a short illusion of being at the beach. If your thing is the mountains, then make an illusion of being there.

When you feel decompressed, it's time for you to start your first exercise. Make a mental picture of yourself. In your picture I need you to see yourself looking to have self-assurance. What would you like self-assurance to achieve for you? How would you like it to make your life more beneficial? That's what the story of your mental picture will be about.

Make your picture as truthful as possible. To the best of your power, you have to make them: Moving; colorized; close; three-d; centered sharply; and typically bright. Try out the following properties of your mental picture to see which one makes it feel the most credible to you:

Attempt putting in a border; attempt making it borderless (like an unframed image); attempt making your picture into a panorama.

Correct your picture so that it feels as true and believable as possible. The more frequently you watch these mental pictures, the more beneficial. Bedtime is a fantabulous time to make these mental pictures.

Brief recap: Self-confidence is a mental attitude that's learned with experiences. Once you have success, you'll tend to expect to be successful. And that anticipation will cause you to get a feeling of self-assurance.

A minute ago we talked about how a coach could help to build up hisboxer's confidence.

Likewise, a girl who's afraid of heights wishes to learn to plunge into aswimming pool from an elevated diving board. So she determines a diving coach who asks her to leap into the pool from the 1st step of the ladder up to the elevated board. The 1st step of the ladder isn't really high, so the girl feels no fright, and she bounds from that step, and lands in the water unscathed.

Following, the coach has her leap from the 2nd step of the ladder, andso on. I believe that you're beginning to comprehend. With every additional step up the ladder, as the young lady was successful on the prior step, and this following step is only somewhat higher then the last, the fright factor is paltry, and the missy expects to be successful. When she leaps in and lands unscathed, the girl's self-confidence grows, and her anticipation of success on the following step up the ladder step-ups. If an individual who has a long history of success andnotions of self-confidence does bomb, they all the same tend to expectsuccess the following time out.

Conversely, when an individual who's weak in the confidence department bombs, they tend to lose self-confidence, and start toanticipate failure, which may become a self-fulfilling prophecy.

Having real self-assurance doesn't mean that you'll be able to accomplish everything. Individuals, who have true confidence, commonly have expectations that are truthful. Even when a few of their expectations are not fulfilled, they go on to be positive and toaccept themselves.

Individuals, who lack self-confidence, tend to depend to a fault on theapproval of other people in order to feel good about themselves. Theytend to prevent taking risks as they fear failure. They frequently put themselves down and tend to discount or brush aside the compliments that they do get.

Does any of this sound familiar to you?

Chapter 8

Mighty Techniques For Formulating
Self-Confidence andBravery

Synopsis

Strategies

Stress your strengths. Give yourself credit for everything you are ableto do. And give yourself credit for each new thing that you're willing to attempt.

Accept chances. Acquire the mental attitude of: I never bomb, as there are NO failures. All the same, occasionally I learn what does notwork, and when I've discovered what does not work in a given state ofaffairs, I may do something else.

Utilize Self-Talk. Utilize self-talk as a chance to counter harmful suppositions. And then, tell yourself to stop and replace more sensiblesuppositions.

For instance, once you catch yourself anticipating perfection, remind yourself that no one may do everything perfectly, and that it's only imaginable to do things to the best of your power. This lets you to live with yourself while still endeavoring to improve.

Self-Assess. Learn to assess yourself independently. Avoid the unceasing sense of chaos that comes from relying too much on thenotions of other people.

Now what I'd wish you to do is to actually compose the answers to the accompanying questions. Individuals, who truly want to successfully formulate self- confidence and bravery, in reality, write the answers down.

1: In what region of your life do you lack self-confidence and bravery?Is it with the opposite sex? Is it in social spots? Is it with your foreman? Is it when you're confronted? Please put down the question,and the answers.

2: Why do you lack self-assurance in this region? May you supply facts or memories to rationalize your deficiency of confidence? Or dothe realities tell you that you're truly a capable individual with negative anticipations?

3: Have you ever truly asked for that date? Or have you in reality asked your foreman for that raise? Or in reality climbed up that mountain? Or did you decline to even try it as you told yourself thatyou could not accomplish it?

If you did in reality ask for the date, or the raise, or try what ever it is that you desired to try, and you bombed, what occurred? Were you wounded? Did it kill you? Are you lifeless? Or did you endure and scarcely make yourself feel bad about it?

As if you survived and you made yourself feel bad about it, there's hope for you, as you're in command. You're in command as you made yourself feel bad. And if you are able to make yourself feel bad, then you are able to likewise make yourself feel all right, or even great about it!

Now I'd like you to work out what your strengths are as relates to thefield that you lack confidence in. And you're going to wish to write these strengths down! For now, brush aside any weak points that youbelieve you might have.

For instance, if you lack self-confidence in social or dating type spots,consider the aspects of your personality that you do feel positive about, that may be associated to social or dating type spots.

Do most individuals find you magnetic? Do most individuals find youto be intriguing, or funny, or well-informed, or insightful? Put down all of your strengths.

Make certain that as you write up your list, you phrase everything in the positive. Put differently, if you're smart, put down: "I am smart." Don't put down: "I am not stupid!" Everything must be formulated insuch a way that, you're telling yourself what you are, rather than whatyou're not!

As an easy illustration, if you desired to tell yourself that you're not standing, how would you do it? Easy, you'd tell yourself that you're seated, or lying down. And if you wanted to tell yourself that you're not anxious, how would you accomplish that? That's easy also; you'dtell yourself that you're at ease! Get the theme?

If you lack self-confidence when it comes to being confronted, whatare your strengths here? Do you commonly only do things that youtrust are the correct things to do? Are you level headed? Do you commonly know what you're talking about?

If you lack self-confidence when it comes to asking for a raise, what are your strengths here? Are you punctual? Are you great at what youdo? Do you work hard, and so forth?

Now I'd like you to study, and re-read your list of strengths 10 times - aloud. Really view the words, and state them aloud 10 times. You'regoing to want you to do this exercise at least once per day for the following twenty-one days.

In the meantime, begin imagining how your life would be better if you felt confident. And you'll feel confident in your power to transform into a confident individual.

Wrapping Up

Our fears impact us physically, mentally and emotionally. They compound our negative thinking and mar our normal perception, reasonableness and comprehension. They make us limit our prospects and avoid taking excessive risks or face ramifications. While our fears are meant to be part of our survival instinct, they get to be a problem when they begin to interfere with our normal functioning.

You are able to overcome your fears nonetheless!

Hopefully this book has presented you the tools to lead you down the proven path of overcoming your fears.

Printed by Libri Plureos GmbH in Hamburg,
Germany

9 784642 506540